Commander and Crew

The Human Factors Approach to

Teambuilding and Leadership

USO 30 LOW C
PD: OBR DRONE

USO 94
ME: TIN MELLW
B & A middle

Commander and Crew

The Human Factors Approach to
Teambuilding and Leadership

The highly regarded training program that is now
available to both Medical and Business leaders.

PETER DENUCCI

Commander and Crew

Address inquiries to the author at:

www.commanderandcrew.com

Published by Booksurge, an amazon.com company.

ISBN 1-4196-1256-5

To order additional copies, please contact us.

BookSurge, LCC
www.booksurge.com
1-866-308-6235
orders@booksurge.com

Dedicated to my family-

The best team I have ever known!

CONTENTS

Introduction   ix

Part One - Situational Awareness

1   What Is Your Operational Archetype?   3

2   Fixation   11

3   Ambiguity   15

4   Complacency   19

5   Distraction   25

Part Two - Teambuilding and Leadership

The Commander and Crew Model

6   New Archetype: New Solutions   37

7   The Workplace Commander:
    Responsibility and Authority   39

8   Plotting Your Course: The Plan   41

9   The Briefing   45

10 The Enrollment: Is Everyone On Board?   47

11 Accepting Command   49

12 The Debrief   53

13 Commander and Crew Courtesies   55

14 The Multi-Generational Workplace   61

15 Faith   63

ACKNOWLEDGMENTS

I would like to especially thank my wife, Beverly, for her continuous love and support during the writing of this book. Your guidance and wisdom, were invaluable.

Of course, a big "thank you" goes out to my fellow professionals who gave their all when it came to sharing their stories in leadership - Don, Tom, Bev, Kurt, and Mark. You know who you are, and I can't thank you enough!

Graphics and design-work credits go to Mark Armbruster and Roger Caplan from the Caplan Group of Columbia, MD. "Thank you, gentlemen!"

Jessica, Pamela, and Suzanne from Booksurge Publishing - what can I say but, "thank you!" While it was your expertise and software knowledge that helped ensure Commander and Crew would reach the printers, it was actually your care and dedication that brought it to those who needed it. Again - "thank you!"

INTRODUCTION
The Need: A Metamorphosis.

It was not long ago when we were witness to some of the worst aircraft accidents in history. As aviation professionals searched for the root causes of these accidents, many avenues were pursued — engineering, design, weather, maintenance, and pilot procedures to name a few. Within time, we discovered that these categories accounted for less that twenty-eight percent of all accidents. With more than seventy-two percent of these deadly crashes being caused by what is now known as "Human Factors" errors, immediate action was required. The industry then catapulted itself into a zero-hull loss standard (zero-accident), as mandated by the Federal Aviation Administration. Thanks to the support of NASA and others, the standard was quickly met. There was an effective culture change, a "culture of safety" — a metamorphosis which would be heralded as one of the most dramatic and permanent evolutions in the American work-place on record. Thousands of lives were saved, as well as the aircraft that transported them.

During my twenty-five years of flying experience, I have been extensively involved in education, flight training, Crew Resource Management, and multi-level Human Factors pro-grams. Despite tremendous resistance brought on by the old archetypes, this new Human Factors science was born. It is a vast body of information designed to help people maintain their leadership roles while establishing communicative environments, build highly effective teams, enhance job per-formance, and execute tasks on demand — especially during high stress situations.

Part One of **Commander and Crew** focuses on the very foundation of Human Factors education — Situational Awareness. This highly regarded program demonstrates first and foremost, that we must be aware of our current environment and the forces acting upon us. This proven curriculum is used to teach pilots how to maintain a clear-eyed perspective in their ever-changing environments. **Commander and Crew** applies this highly efficient method to everyday workplace scenarios, thereby empowering us with the heightened state of awareness required for implementation of the very successful five-step model, which is explained in Part Two of this book.

Let's take a look at a few key concepts that will be presented in detail in later chapters.

Situational Awareness: The accurate perception or knowledge a Commander maintains of the operational environment in order to anticipate contingencies and take necessary actions. In other words, having the big picture at all times.

If you are to take command of your crew (team), you must have an understanding of how your current situation came to be. You must be aware of the forces that helped manifest it. With situational awareness, you will have the big picture, and understand your role.

Quite often it is our operational archetype, which actually prevents us from achieving the situational awareness we need. Because we tend to cling to our own model of the world, our reality may not include the required awareness, and therefore, we may never really be able to anticipate what's in store for us, or our crew. We find ourselves reacting to our environment rather than implementing an effective plan, and are then surprised when our team is hesitant to follow us. (They always know who is at the helm.)

Ironically, if you lose situational awareness, you never seem to miss it...until it's too late! After all, if you are not aware of something you have, you will not miss it when it is gone. For this reason, you will be trained to recognize symptoms, which may occur with a loss of situational awareness. These are called "Red Flags", and when they pop up, they warn you that a loss of situational awareness is not far behind.

RED FLAGS

Fixation: The focus of attention on any one item to the exclusion of all others. Often we fixate on day-to-day events which have nothing to do with where we need to take our crew, so we lose the broader perspective.

Ambiguity: Two or more independent sources of information that do not agree. For example, our operational archetype can have multiple levels of authority (too many bosses) and we can easily get lost in the confusion.

Complacency: A feeling that everything is going well, based only on the fact that we have done it before. In other words, it is a comfort borne of familiarity. Sometimes, everything is going along just fine, but at other times we may be ignoring an important hidden issue.

Distraction: A sudden turning away from the original focus of attention. We can become so engrossed in putting out daily fires that we forget our overall mission.

In effect, these Red Flags signal us that some aspect of our environment needs attention. We can then take the necessary action to fully restore our situational awareness.

PART ONE

SITUATIONAL AWARENESS

CHAPTER ONE
What is your operational archetype?

The Boeing 777 is one of the most modern passenger jets in the world today. It can carry 375 people at speeds up to 588 mph, or nearly the speed of sound. It has a cruise range of over 8,300 miles and can fly at altitudes over 35,000 feet, while burning less fuel than any comparable model previously introduced. The engines are capable of developing 100,000 lbs of thrust each, the highest in the industry. Due to its high level of cockpit automation, the Boeing 777 requires only two pilots.

Today, one of these pilots is Captain Charles Hansen, and for the first time, he will be allowed to actually fly from one city to another. Having just passed his rigorous "checkride," in which he demonstrated his sharp piloting skills, he is now looking forward to a routine flight. With many years of experience flying B-727s, Captain Hansen enthusiastically waits to command all of this new technology.

After getting tower clearance for take-off, Hansen advances the throttles to the stand-up position, and allows several seconds for the goliath turbo-fans to spool up. He engages the auto-throttles, thus commanding the computer to fine-tune the power setting. The huge jet responds to the 200,000 lbs of thrust, and begins accelerating down the runway. In a matter of seconds, Hansen removes his hand from the nose wheel tiller, and begins steering with his feet. The rudder responds, allowing him to keep this speeding 200 tons centered on the runway. In fact, he can even feel the recessed centerline lights making that familiar thump against the nose wheels.

When the airspeed indicator reaches 137 knots, First Officer

Steve Willis, calls out, "V1." Hansen is now aware that he has reached what is known as the "decision speed," which means there is not enough runway remaining to abort the take-off. From this point forward, he is committed to getting the B-777 airborne.

Following procedure, Willis calls out "Rotate." This is Hansen's signal to begin easing back on the yoke, to lift the big jet off the runway.

As they climb through 1,000 feet, Hansen calls out various commands to his First Officer. Following orders, Willis retracts the plane's flaps, and updates the Flight Management Computers. They also check with Air Traffic Control (ATC) about the required altitudes and headings.

Climbing out of 5,000 feet, Hansen initiates a right turn to a heading of 90 degrees. He accelerates to 250 knots, and levels off at 7,000 feet. This action maneuvers their aircraft into the clouds, and they are now flying solely on instruments.

ATC: "Twin-Jet 211, fly heading 110, and climb and maintain 9,000 feet. You have traffic at two o'clock and 15 miles at 10,000 feet. Expect clearance to flight level 230 when clear of traffic."

Willis: "Roger, Twin-Jet 211."

As Hansen begins his climb to 9,000 feet, he notices the sudden illumination of the generator fault light for the number two engine. This indicates that the aircraft has lost half its normal electrical source. Though the generator on the number one engine will pick up most of the load, he needs a back-up source of electrical power.

Hansen: "Steve, start the Auxiliary Power Unit (APU), and call out the emergency checklist procedures."

Willis: "I'm starting the APU now. Standby for the generator failure checklist."

ATC: "Twin-Jet 211, you have traffic 1,000 feet above you. Do you have them in sight yet?"

There is no answer on the radio.

The flight attendant's call bell breaks the silent concentration in the cockpit.

Hansen: "Ignore that bell for now, just read the checklist, and when you're done, tell the company we're returning to Portland."

Willis: "Ok, Generator Failure Checklist. One — APU start and on line. Two — Deselect inoperative generator. Three — Select..."

It is while Willis continues reading that the flight attendant's call bell rings again.

ATC: "Twin-Jet 211, traffic two o'clock, four miles, 10,000 feet. They will not be a factor. Go ahead and call Seattle Center on frequency 125.7 and they'll give you a higher altitude as soon as you're clear of that traffic. Have a good flight."

Hansen is not overly concerned with ATC at this moment; he knows the traffic is 1,000 feet above him, and they have a safe, legal separation. He is concerned with the current emergency. His first priority is to restore the electrical power!

Hansen: "Continue with the checklist..."

Once again, the flight attendant's call bell rings.

Hansen is now starting to feel the pressure. Everyone is calling on him at once. He turns on the autopilot allowing the plane fly itself, so he can focus on getting electrical power back up to the normal output.

Willis: "Verify volts on... ah, Hansen, did you verify the volts...?"

More ringing.

Hansen: "Damn it, answer that flight attendant call bell, so they stop calling us! We have an emergency up here!"

Willis: "This is Steve, we have an emergency. We are going to return to Portland. Get the passengers ready."

Junior Flight Attendant: (trying to conceal her nervousness) "Steve, the galley power is out, and the lights on the left side of the plane don't work. We'll get everybody ready!"

Hansen: "All right now, let's finish that checklist!"

Meanwhile the flight attendants are meeting in the forward galley to employ their emergency procedures.

Lead Flight Attendant: (to the junior flight attendant who called the cockpit) "I know the Captain told you we have an emergency, but did he specifically tell you to prepare for an evacuation and what the brace signal would be?"

Junior Flight Attendant: "No, he just said we have an emergency and are returning to Portland. They sounded really busy up there."

Lead Flight Attendant: "Let's start preparing the cabin now. I'll have to talk to the Captain eventually, to find out if he wants to order an evacuation when we land."

Willis: "Five — electrical output..."

Willis and Hansen finish the checklist, and the airplane now has sufficient electrical energy to run all the systems normally.

Hansen: "All right, we are back in business. Now did you call company operations and tell them we are coming back?"

Willis: "No, but I'll do it right now."

The ringing starts again.

Hansen: "I thought you already told the flight attendants what was going on! Tell them again — we have an emergency!"

As Willis selects the intercom to talk with the flight attendant, he hears the sickening computer yelp of the ground proximity warning system.

"TERRAIN! TERRAIN! TERRAIN!"

"PULL UP! PULL UP! PULL UP!"

Though the pilots are initially confused, they both yank back on the yoke, hoping to climb above whatever is out there; after all, they were still at 9,000 feet. What was going on?

As the airplane hit Mount Rainier, the cockpit shook a little, and the altimeter wound back down to Portland airport elevation. The cockpit door opens, and the calming voice of Captain Paul Kennedy fills the void. "Well, Hansen, looks like you just flew a B-777 into Mount Rainier. Let's get out of this simulator and go to the debriefing room."

This airline had implemented Human Factors training, and in this case, the simulated flight was designed to overload the pilot. With the aid of appropriate feedback, Hansen would be able to see exactly what he did, and the consequences of that action. He would actually be able to examine the cause-effect of Human Factors-related cockpit communication.

During this debriefing, a pilot will witness first hand what happens when situational awareness is lost. They will experience it. In this case, Hansen lost situational awareness and flew into the mountain. The Red Flags were fixation and distraction. Captain Hansen will learn to recognize these Red Flags, as well as the importance of utilizing his crew to their full capability.

There will be no one telling him that his crew resource management skills needed improvement. He will learn that effective communication with other crewmembers is now part of the job. Afterwards, he will come to an understanding that under the high pressure and intense stress of the first flight emergency, he reverted back to his lone-ranger instincts. Captain Hansen tried to handle everything by himself, while giving orders that his team could not follow.

It will be a true self-debriefing for this Captain. He will shortly be offered several new Human Factors skills — now that he has decided he wants them.

The cause-effect relationship of human behavior is an interesting phenomenon. Whenever we do or say something, there is a response from our environment. When a certain behavior elicits an immediate effect, it is easy for us to see this cause-effect relationship.

When the response is not immediate, we sometimes lose the correlation between the cause and its effect. We find ourselves wondering why certain things are manifesting in a particular fashion.

8

A good analogy is thrust control in the cockpit of an airliner. When a pilot moves the throttles, it can take up to ten seconds for the engines to develop the selected thrust. The huge size of the turbine engines requires this time to spool up. A well-trained pilot knows the time-span between throttle movement and engine thrust, i.e., the necessary cause-effect relationship.

This is why pilots are trained to understand the results of any input into their flight. Knowing that certain inputs will take longer to manifest than others, especially those related to Human Factors, is essential to understanding situational awareness.

Situational awareness is an ally, which will allow anyone to implement corrections in their workplace, and get their team back on course. Being alert to the Red Flags will help maintain this state. Remember, we may not recognize the loss of situational awareness, until it's too late.

CHAPTER TWO
Fixation

It is another serene evening in southern Florida. The weather is perfect, as the Jumbo L-1011 jet is cleared for final approach into Miami International. A tired crew has just finished safely navigating their way back home. This is the landing all three pilots have been waiting for, as its completion means the end of a four-day trip and time with their families. Everyone wants to get home.

Captain: "Miami tower, this is Tri-Jet 301, on the visual approach for runway niner."

Miami Tower: "Tri-Jet 301, this is Miami tower, you are cleared to land on runway niner."

Captain: "Roger, Tri-Jet 301 is cleared to land on runway niner."

The First Officer selects the gear handle to the down position. Only two of the three green lights become illuminated. The crew cannot verify that all the wheels are down — they will have to execute a go-around, and circle the airport for another attempted landing.

Captain: "Ah, Miami, it looks like we have a gear problem ... probably just a light bulb. We'll have to execute a go around and take a look at this."

Miami Tower: "Roger Tri-Jet 301, fly heading 090... and climb to 2,000 feet."

Captain: "Roger. Climb to 2,000 feet, heading 090. Tri-Jet 301."

The big jet heads out over the Florida Everglades, allowing

the crew more time to solve the problem. The Captain levels the L-1011 at 2,000 feet and activates the autopilot. Now they are able to troubleshoot.

As any experienced pilot knows, most landing gear problems are not actually in the gear itself, but in the indication system, such as a switch or a simple light bulb. This well-seasoned crew takes the appropriate course of action and attempts to replace the light bulb first. If successful, they will obviously not have to employ more extensive emergency procedures.

But something unexpected happens during this relatively simple procedure. The first officer cannot remove the snap-in bulb! The Captain joins in the effort but with no success. Because of the immediate nature and apparent simplicity of the emergency, both pilots and the engineer are soon trying to remedy the situation. All their energy is focused on one small problem. Fixation occurs and situational awareness decays. While working on the light bulb, one of the pilots gently bumps the yoke (flight controls) and starts an unrecognizable descent into the treacherous everglades below. The result is catastrophic. Tri-Jet 301 leaves Miami's radar screen and is never heard from again.

Fixation can be deadly!

Though this accident resulted from the loss of situational awareness, the initial cause was fixation. The crew was not aware of their airplane's collision course with the everglades because all of their attention was focused on one aspect of their environment. They lost sight of the big picture.

Until you are intimately familiar with what situational awareness feels like, you probably will not recognize its absence. This is why we have warning signs and Red Flags.

When a pilot dwells on one procedure for an extended period, he becomes aware that he is fixating. More importantly, he realizes that loss of situational awareness is not far behind. So a pilot is trained to recognize fixation, thus allowing him to take the necessary action in a timely fashion.

Fixation, however, is not limited to the cockpits of airliners. It finds its way into our daily lives as well. Whether it manifests itself in our business world, healthcare facilities, or personal relationships, fixation always leads us down the same road and creates the same result: the loss of situational awareness! Let's take a look at an actual medical scenario.

Linda is a thoughtful, conscientious, and talented Nurse Anesthetist. She enjoys her job, and gives her best everyday. But due to the large volume of patients, some of those days find her with quite a challenge. Her doctors depend on her to prep their patients, while the resident nurses look to her for that extra attention she usually gives them during the "on-the-job" coaching. Today, she will again do her best, but an inadequate operational archetype will cause her and the resident nurse to fail...

A young man is being prepped for surgery. After purposefully rendering the thirty-year-old patient unconscious, Linda instructs a new resident nurse to set up the arterial line (similar to an IV). Feeling as though most of the difficult prep has been completed, Linda leaves the arterial task with the resident, and devotes her needed attention to a more pressing need with a patient nearby.

While working on the arterial line, the resident nurse confronts some difficulty. He cannot get the IV to flow! He proceeds to make several other attempts, but does not have any luck. As he continues fixating on the arterial line, he becomes unaware that the patient is no longer receiving oxygen through the oxygen tube. Though the monitor is displaying low levels, which would lead to hypoxia, he is not watching the screen. By the time the error is found, it is too late. The patient developed irreversible severe brain damage as the result of oxygen deprivation, and never regained consciousness.

Again, fixation must be recognized early! This is required to prevent the loss of Situational Awareness. Though some would simply choose to play the blame game in the analysis of this scenario, this unfortunately will not change any of the procedures. If we are to decrease the probability of an incident-repeat, the addition of checklists and human factors training becomes very useful. The checklists establish the predetermined focus, and the Human Factors training allows two or more individuals to keep that like-focus, thus elevating their awareness to any of the Red Flags. The chances of an incident-repeat are dramatically reduced.

CHAPTER THREE
Ambiguity

First Officer: "Looks like we have a line of showers between us and Chicago."

Captain: "I read the weather report before we left and it said there might be some precipitation. We should be able to get a good picture of any heavy areas with the airborne radar."

The DC-9 is now level at 24,000 feet, cruising at 500 mph. Things begin happening fast — maybe too fast. The line of thunderstorms that the Captain read about before departure had swelled into a solid line of water, hail, and wind shear. Conditions have dramatically changed.

The weather radar installed on the DC-9 is capable of showing precipitation ahead of its path and alerting the crew of expected ride conditions. Normally, an image of the rain shower would be displayed on the pilot's radar screen, but if the precipitation is too heavy, the radar beam will not able to penetrate the edge of the storm. This results in the illusionary display of a thin, harmless band of rain. Consequently, the area that appears to be the safest on radar, can very well be the most dangerous to fly through. This is known as "radar attenuation."

First Officer: "It looks like a heading of 080 should take us through the lightest part of the storm."

Captain: "I agree. The radar is showing a pretty good ride there. It's kind of funny the way that narrow band of weather is right where we need it. This radar is great."

First Officer: "Sure makes it easy to penetrate a line..."

Within two minutes, the DC-9 slams into a solid wall of water; the golf-ball size hail flames out both engines and shatters the outer panes of both pilots' windshields. In desperation, the Captain wrestles with the flight controls until the last possible moment. A cornfield is picked as the emergency landing area, but later proves to be too rough for the DC-9. The results are tragic.

A crash similar to this happened many years ago when aircraft radar was still in its infancy. Common knowledge with regard to its operation was limited at best. Man simply did not know enough about thunderstorms and their corresponding relationship on radar.

During the early years of the jet age, ambiguity was indeed a problem. Pilots experienced the influx of new information, or environmental data, which did not always agree with old data. The eventual loss of situational awareness could then lead to degraded safety margins.

In the cockpit of an airliner, where a pilot is constantly processing information, ambiguity must be eliminated as quickly as possible. For example: when dealing with dangerous weather, the Commander must check many available sources regarding the flight path. These sources may include the National Weather Service, the airline, Air Traffic Control, on-board radar, and even other pilots. Then, based on all this information, an enhanced decision must be made. Remember, every piece of data received up to this point is true and valid in the reality of the sender. It is up to the Commander to find the connection behind all these reports so that he or she can have a safe flight.

Again, the only way to truly clear up ambiguity of any type is to identify one source of information as incorrect and eliminate it; or discover the connection behind those different sources and come to an enhanced decision. With this latter type of decision, derived from fully processing new information, we may enter a new operational archetype. This is an archetype with which there is no ambiguity, leaving us in a state of situational awareness.] ᔕTᴏᵖ

Anyone who is confronted with two or more independent sources of information, which do not agree with each other, can experience ambiguity. For example, in the complicated world of business, a loss of situational awareness can be brought on by a poor operational archetype in the area of authority. In other words — "who's the boss?" Let's take a look at an actual problem that a friend of mine, Debbie (not her real name) experienced.

Debbie is a dedicated employee, and a valuable member of a growing company. Her daily activities include the managing of a rather large staff. This particular staff is very intelligent and scientifically minded. Many of them tend to remain steeped in their work, and because they deal with the broad technical interests of the company, several different divisions call on them from time to time. This creates an interesting scenario for Debbie. Without her knowing, other managers may call on her team members, and because they are rather reserved, she may not get the feedback she needs to effectively manage. Though she has developed a method for keeping the lines of communication open with them, it does take some effort. On an average day, things seem to go along just fine.

But today is different. Debbie receives a task from her immediate division chief, which is in conflict with another division chief who is leading an ad-hoc mission utilizing over half of her team members. Both division chiefs have important missions, and they both think that theirs is more important to the long-term interests of the company.

This obviously creates a very ambiguous situation for Debbie. She is the "Commander" of her team or "Crew" and yet she is also a "Crewmember" of the larger company team. What can she do? Remember, the information is always true in the reality of the sender — both division chiefs think they are right.

Debbie can (and did) get to an enhanced decision with both bosses. She gathered all the data she possibly could from each chief, and created a plan that would work for **both** of them, then she followed through and implemented this plan with **her** team. The five-step process, or **Commander and Crew Model** is discussed in greater detail in Part Two of this book.

CHAPTER FOUR
Complacency

Robbie is fueling his last plane tonight. Today's total was thirty-five aircraft and 1,640 gallons of 100LL (a low lead fuel). In this small commuter operation he can handle up to 150 Cessna-402 aircraft in one week. The work is tough, dirty, and smelly. But if he keeps up a good pace he can usually stay on schedule. He also fuels an occasional turbo-prop when it pulls into the gate. Robbie is good at what he does, and the pilots can depend on him to be there with the fuel needed.

In a few moments, Captain Thomas Erickson will need eighty gallons of 100LL — but that is not what he'll get.

As Tom taxies his Cessna-402 into the gate, his passengers are anxious to deplane. As soon as all ten are escorted into the terminal, five more excited travelers are ready for departure. The courteous, busy gate agent begins collecting the new tickets.

"Forty gallons in each tank!" commands Captain Erickson, making sure he is heard above the ramp noise. In a small operation like this, it is up to the pilot to tell the fueler personally the number of gallons he needs.

"OK Tom, you're number three tonight. I'll get you in a few minutes!" Robbie is moving fast. Two turbo-props just came in and needed 100 gallons of JET-A. He had to finish them first. No problem. After all, he'd done this a hundred times.

Tom quickly heads into the flight operations room and takes another look at the weather, just to be sure there aren't new thunderstorms developing. Even though he's been flying all afternoon, it is always a good idea to double-check the latest forecast. The flight release is the next document to review and after verifying everything, he leaves his signature with the operations agent.

Having completed all his preflight checks, Tom straps himself into the pilot's seat and waits for his passengers. The boarding process goes smoothly and before long everyone is settled in, listening to the Cessna-402 safety brief. There are no flight attendants on these smaller planes, so Tom makes all the announcements while taxiing. After receiving take-off clearance, the little twin-engine plane starts down the runway.

With flaps and gear up, Erickson initiates a turn for his first navigation fix. Before he and his passengers even have time to admire the beautiful Florida scenery, Tom notices the left engine overheating. As he starts to reduce power, he notices the right engine beginning to overheat. In less than a minute the two engines are so hot that fire is imminent. Tom commands the aircraft to bank left and locks on a heading for an emergency landing back at the departure airport. But, as he attempts radio contact with the tower, the left engine bursts into flames. He cannot wait any longer — he has to shut it down, now!

"THROTTLE — IDLE."

"MIXTURE — CUT OFF."

"PROPELLER — FEATHER."

Erickson goes through the drill as he's been trained to do. Except this time, he has to shut down both engines — within seconds the right engine will be so hot the alloy block will start melting! He repeats the drill:

"THROTTLE — IDLE."

"MIXTURE — CUTOFF."

"PROPELLER — FEATHER."

There is no way he can make the airport now; he has to pick a nearby field. Anything about a thousand feet long, no power lines, not too rough ...

With just a slight heading change he finds himself set up for a small cow pasture. He will aim for that.

After a successful landing, the right wing of the Cessna-402 cracks open, spilling fuel on the hot engine. The ensuing fire blocks off the right emergency exit, leaving only the two left exits. Miraculously, Captain Erickson is able to evacuate all but one passenger. As he guides everyone to a safe meeting place amidst the blazing aluminum inferno, confusion begins to set in. What on earth happened?

The answer was easy to find.

While Tom was signing his paperwork in operations, Robbie accidentally fueled his airplane with JET-A, a fuel very similar to kerosene, which burns at too high a temperature for reciprocating engines (piston). Both engines literally melted.

Complacency has affected all of us at one time or another. It is a natural human tendency to relax focus and concentration on job tasks, once we have mastered them. If we can recognize this behavior, we can prevent loss of situational awareness. In aviation Human Factors, we study these accidents to learn from them. Afterwards, we can install the proper safeguards to prevent their reoccurrence. We do not blame; we look for root causes. By studying one accident, we can prevent ten in the future.

Complacency can creep into our operational archetypes, concealing itself behind many areas that we do not suspect: policies and procedures, competitive naivety, and simple inadequate "upward" communication, just to name a few.

These particular types of complacency, if not recognized in their early stages, will result in the loss of situational awareness. Let's take a look at another true scenario ...

Dr. Jacobs (not his actual name) is one of Maryland's most respected orthopedic surgeons. Having earned the title of Chief of Surgery of a prestigious group practice, he enjoys the admiration and respect of several neighboring hospitals. His fellow professionals relish the opportunity to serve as a member of his operating team.

Today, Beth, a very nervous, but trusting young woman, is reporting for surgery. After years of daily jogging she developed degenerative joint disease in her left knee. She arrives for her surgical appointment as scheduled and successfully completes the necessary preoperative tasks which include a physical examination, interview by an anesthesiologist, and a review of her past and present medical history. Everything seems routine thus far.

The caring nurses administer the sedatives, and Beth begins feeling very relaxed. This helps ease the tension, as the anesthetist connects the IV to administer the anesthetic. Soon Dr. Jacobs enters the room and begins a comforting chat with the young patient. As Beth begins to drift off, she hears someone say, "Okay let's get her right knee prepped..." Fortunately Beth is not fully sedated, and is able to advise the team that it is her left knee that requires surgery, not her right.

Complacency is a quiet killer, and therefore it is one of the most difficult red flags to recognize. Someone on this team nearly prepped the incorrect knee for surgery. When multiple people in a chain are required to transfer information, there must be an adequate communications network in place. This "comms-net" must have checklists that are designed and implemented for each phase of personal integration, otherwise situational awareness will decay.

CHAPTER FIVE
Distraction

PROBLEM

"This is the Springfield weather — two thousand overcast, visibility two miles, winds are calm, altimeter 29.97. Runway 9 left approach in use. Taxiway delta and taxiway alpha are closed."

Travis did not have to listen to the remainder of the Springfield advisory tape. He knew those taxiways were closed; after all, most of his 256 hours of flight time were logged right here in Springfield. He even knew the airport frequencies from memory. Having just passed his Instrument Rating Checkride, he was now legally qualified to fly an instrument approach without an Instructor on board. He wanted to log every approach he could schedule. Travis knew each minute of actual instrument flight time was pure gold in his pilot's logbook. He loved to fly the Mooney aircraft on instruments, as it was a quick little plane that offered a challenge — a sports car with wings.

SAVE

Travis: "Springfield approach, this is Mooney seven niner gulf, I am ten miles north at 4,500 feet squawking one two zero zero."

Approach Control: "Roger, Mooney seven niner gulf, squawk code three two four five."

Travis enters the new code into the transponder. This identifies his airplane on the radar screen. After air traffic control has a positive radar return, he is told to descend to 1,600 feet and fly an intercept heading for the approach. Quickly, he reviews the instrument approach plate. He wants to be well prepared for this landing. Those instruments are going to be right on center! As he nears the runway, approach control hands him off to the tower.

Travis: "Springfield Tower, this is Mooney seven niner gulf, on approach, runway 9 left."

No response from the tower.

Travis: "Ah tower. This is Mooney seven niner gulf, runway 9 left."

Tower: "Roger, Mooney seven niner gulf, continue. Expect clearance to land shortly."

Travis: "Roger, seven niner gulf."

As Travis descends through 1,200 feet, he struggles to get the airplane back on center. The four seater is doing a pretty good job of staying on course, but Travis wants it nailed; he wants it to be exact. Those extra radio calls on the approach didn't help things because he had to keep picking up the microphone.

"OK, that looks better. Got her nailed! Now for the landing checklist. Mixture... prop..."

Tower: "Mooney seven niner gulf, I may have to break you off the approach, ah, are you getting a good signal for the approach?"

Travis: "Springfield, this is seven niner gulf, I just lost the instrument landing signal, but I have the runway in sight."

Tower: "OK, seven niner gulf, you are cleared to land on runway 9 right, I say again, 9 right."

Travis: "Roger, cleared to land runway 9 right."

Travis has his hands full now — he had to break off the approach for 9 left and line up his plane on 9 right. He had practiced this sidestep maneuver before, but not alone and certainly not in these conditions. He commands a hard bank to the right, followed by a hard bank back to the left. The new runway begins filling the windscreen. Travis now has to employ the short field landing technique, which means flying at a slower speed and stabilizing the glide path just above the tree line at the approach end of this short runway. The landing point is selected; the speed is locked on 85 knots. His glide path is perfect. As he enters his flair, he slowly retards the throttle, holding the nose off. ...

Tower: "Hey, ah, Mooney seven niner gulf, check your landing gear...!"

SCREEEECH!!!

Although Travis nailed the instrument approach and successfully maneuvered the airplane to runway 9 right, he forgot a very important requirement to facilitate a smooth safe landing. He had not extended his landing gear! Having been distracted several times during his approach, he never actually completed the final landing checklist. The items that distracted him were valid and important events, which are legitimate aspects of a pilot's environment. They required and demanded his attention, but not to the exclusion of his other duties.

Similarly, distraction can cause a loss of situational awareness for a group of people, whether they are a family, a corporate team, or even a three-person flight crew.

***

Stanberry is a small town in the Carolinas that used its Southern charm over the years to attract new business: boundless land for development, a low tax base, and a country smile to boot. Top it all off with a moderate climate, and you've baited the hook for some new neighbors. And they came running.

The United States military also had plans for Stanberry, as they had decided to increase the military budgets, and expand some of the smaller army bases. For Stanberry, this meant a boost to the local economy, and the necessity for increased airline service. The small local airport would have to be renovated, as would the military airport on the other side of town, at least twelve miles away. Let's take a look at this three-person crew ...

The Boeing 727 streaks across the Carolina night sky, the mountains below offering no sign of a resting place. In the distance, maybe fifty miles or so, there is the faint glimmer of streetlights. Traveling at eight miles a minute, the crew would be on top of Stanberry in no time.

First Officer: "I sure wish the Stanberry VOR (ground navigation instrument) was in service, it would make it a lot easier to find this place. I'm going to try to pick up another signal."

Captain: "Okay, you try to lock on that and I'll ask Approach for vectors. You'd think we could see it by now, being a clear night and all."

First Officer: "This signal isn't strong enough for navigation either, must be the mountains."

Captain (on radio): "Approach, we can't seem to get a good navigation signal tonight. How about a heading for Stanberry?"

ATC: "Roger, fly heading one five zero, and you should pick up the airport at twelve o'clock.... twenty four miles."

Captain: "Heading one five zero, and we're looking for the field."

First Officer: "Hey, I think I just saw the airport beacon ... there ... about twelve o'clock and twenty miles."

Captain: "I have the airport in sight and the runway lights also. Looks like a north-south configuration, yep that's it. That's got to be runway one eight ...."

"Ding, ding, ding," (the flight attendant's call bell)

Second Officer: "This is Rick, what's the problem?"

Flight Attendant: "There's a weird noise coming from this back service door. It's a whistling sound."

Second Officer: "Don't worry, it's probably just air leaking through the door seal because we're descending. These old 727's do that sometimes, but we'll check it on the ground anyway.... which will be in about five minutes."

Captain: "What did the flight attendant want? Is there a problem in the back of the plane?"

Second Officer: "No problem, just a service door leak. I told them we'd take a look at it on the ground — unless you want me to go back there now, and check it out?"

Captain: "No, we can check that on the ground. And besides, we need you up here to help look for a Cessna between us and the airport. Approach is not talking to him and he might be lost."

First Officer: "I got him... two o'clock... I don't think he'll be a factor."

Captain: "Good, tell Approach we have the traffic, and the airport in sight. And Rick, you tell Operations in Stanberry to have maintenance standing by to have a look at that aft service door. Give me flaps, five degrees."

First Officer: (While selecting flaps five degrees for the Captain) "Stanberry Approach, we have the traffic and the airport in sight."

Approach: "Roger, you are released to Unicom frequency 122.8. Call me on the ground to cancel flight plan."

NOTE: Because some airports are not large enough to have FAA control towers, a Unicom or Universal Communication frequency would be used. This is the frequency that pilots use to talk to each other and to notify each other of their intentions.

Captain: "Gear down... Landing checklist..."

The pilots complete all pre-landing checks, and the Captain rolls the big jet onto the runway for a smooth landing. As he clears the runway, and the first officer finishes the after-landing checklist, he gets a sickening feeling inside. He stops the 727 on the taxiway and sets the parking brake. Just then, the first officer looks up and shouts, "Hey, why are all these military planes parked here?"

A scenario very similar to this happened several years ago. The flight crew was distracted during their final descent into a small southeast airport and landed at the wrong destination. The items that distracted them were valid and important events. The incidents required and demanded their attention.

Valid and important events can also distract us in our personal and business lives. We can invest time and energy in

Read →

30

operational archetypes, which will never get us to our destination. We relinquish our situational awareness because we are too busy putting out fires. Once again, we lose sight of the big picture.

The key is to effectively lead your crew now. It is the best way to prevent landing at the wrong airport, only to find out your crew (team) doesn't have enough fuel to go on to the real destination.

PART TWO

Teambuilding and Leadership:
The Commander and Crew Model

CHAPTER SIX
New Archetype: New Solutions.

The aforementioned aviation stories are based on a combination of actual incidents that happened at real airlines — that no longer exist. Through the dedicated and in-depth research of these "high-stress human interactions," several Human Factors training programs, such as Crew Resource Management, and the Advanced Qualification Program (AQP), were developed.

These Human Factors skills and philosophies are integrated into the airline-training environments, and are the only acceptable basis for doing business today. There is a very prominent difference between this type of workplace and the previously prevalent environment of Total Quality Management. It is simply this — the Commander's role is not only left intact, but the duties are enhanced to the level where interpersonal skills are now an essential part of the job. Commanders must consciously create environments that foster the crewmembers' desire to participate with the self-assuredness to input their front-line data. This type of cooperation is paramount in Human Factors training!

In Chapter 14, "The Multi-Generational Workplace," we will discuss why this new type of Commander and Crew leadership is now more appropriate than ever before. Furthermore, as we begin Part II, we will discover the significant relevance and application to other industries.

CHAPTER SEVEN
The Workplace Commander:
Responsibility and Authority

According to Federal Aviation Regulation 91.3, "The pilot in command is directly responsible for, and is the final authority as to, the operation of the aircraft."

What I've always found fascinating about this definition is that the Federal Aviation Administration clearly places responsibility before authority. The Captain must first accept full responsibility for the operation of an aircraft — then he or she will be empowered with the authority to command it.

When we accept full responsibility for our crew, then and only then, will we be empowered to be the Commander.

We're not talking about a limited concept here; a true Commander must have certain core values and principles that he or she brings to the workplace. These values and principles are at the center of the Commander and Crew Model. They can be divided into two main traits — **character and competence**. If a Commander is lacking in one of these areas, the crew will not be able to follow. These are core traits, and they are both required. Let me explain.

If your team is to function effectively it must have the element of trust, which permeates through its membership. This trust must exist among the crewmembers themselves, and in their relationships with the Commander. The Commander creates this team "state of trust" by being trustworthy. This trustworthy behavior is the result of not only having high character and integrity, but also having the required competence to get the job done. You need both.

Just ask yourself the following question: would you want to fly as a passenger on a jet with a really nice guy of high character, who only has a private pilot's license? Or then again, would you elect to have surgery by a doctor who is quite skilled, and yet gambles with his family savings? The fact of the matter is we naturally look for both character and competence in people who have leadership roles.

CHAPTER EIGHT
Plotting Your Course: The Plan.

82

Modern jet airliners navigate using Inertial Reference Systems (IRS). These navigation systems are capable of guiding an aircraft along its intended route of flight with very accurate precision. They are comprised of computers, laser-beam gyroscopic comparators, and visual displays for the pilot, all working in harmony to let the aircraft know its location at any given time. It is capable of providing this data without any external navigation signals. It will always know where it is, assuming it is programmed correctly.

There are several steps to programming the IRS, but they can be classified into three main procedures:

1. Enter current position.

2. Enter final destination.

3. Enter intended route of flight.

The computer must know the aircraft's current position, before anything else can happen. The pilot must program the exact latitude and longitude into the system, thus enabling the aircraft to compute any motion from that start-ing point. When this is done correctly, the laser-beam gyros will then be able to compute the slightest movement. If the pilot enters an incorrect starting point, by missing one digit in the latitude or longitude, the aircraft will actually think it is at a false location and begin its computations. This is why at least two pilots always double-check all programming.

Years ago, however, there was a Korean 747 shot down over Soviet airspace because it was off course. The strongest theory to date suggests that the IRS computers were programmed incorrectly.

The next step to programming the IRS computer is to enter the destination. Again, the computer will need accurate information.

Finally, the pilot will enter the intended route of flight. We use the word "intended" as there may be some minor adjustments along the way, and our route may have to be updated. Being flexible, while still accomplishing the mission, is an important trait of a good Commander.

The route of flight is how we expect to get to our destination. As we program it, we estimate our fuel burns, and time/distance requirements for the various checkpoints as we pass them. We want to be sure we are going to make our destination with the correct fuel on board. Even though we may forecast the winds and weather to be of a certain value, sometimes conditions can change. By utilizing situational awareness, our experience can still be a good one, with everyone arriving safe and sound at the desired destination. Now, let's take a look at your mission.

Check Current Status

Log your point of origin, i.e.... the current status of your crew. Who are they? What resources do they bring to the mission? What are their relationships with their various colleagues and other departments? Get an accurate picture of your current resources, and identify your destination at this point. Remember, you are the Commander and you will give a brief to your crew on this plan later.

Clarify Intended Route

Come up with a general "course" of action that you would like to see this mission follow. Write it down.

Be sure that it is attainable. You may change it later, as your crew feeds you data along the way, but for now this is it. Create a method for measuring your success along the way. In other words, are your resources from step one being utilized effectively, and are you getting closer to your destination? Decide right now what the timeline will be.

Identify Capabilities

List the strengths of each crewmember, and their expected mission assignments. Keep track of your available technology and plan on maximizing it.

Be Aware of Bad Weather

Plan on needing more "fuel" or resources than expected. You want back-ups for all of your assets, whenever possible. Identify an alternate route, and have it ready.

If you maintained your situational awareness during this planning period, you will deliver a confident brief to your crew, and give them a plan of which they are worthy. The quality of your plan and brief, is paramount in creating the trust in you as a Commander.

CHAPTER NINE
The Briefing

An effective briefing is much more than simply sharing the plan with your crew. It is the fundamental establishment of the team, as a cohesive group. As the Commander, you are setting the stage for your effective leadership. You are setting the tone. You have developed the initial "flight-plan," and are now ready to create an effective "micro-culture."

Set The Stage

Show up on time and look sharp. Dress the part. Be prepared. Articulate with clarity and concern, utilizing the Commander and Crew Courtesies (outlined later in this book). The crew desires a high-caliber leader and they will follow you.

Identify Destination and Mission

Clearly state objectives of the mission. Build confidence by emphasizing the attainability of reaching the destination. Share the timeline, the checkpoints, and the need for them.

Share Intended Route

Layout the general direction for take-off, and give the first action items. Spell out the measurement system. Establish the protocols and norms for crewmember communications, and their associated chains of command.

Share the Expected Weather — The Good and the Bad

Let your crew know what kind of ride they are in for. You are preparing them to succeed in the mission.

Highlight the unknown variables. Point out the competitor's strengths and weaknesses.

Create the Trust

Share procedures for exchanging information, and attaining resources. Make sure your crew knows you are dependable and will support them. Live up to your promises!

Share the Alternate Route

Build confidence by sharing a back-up flight-plan. This will let your crew know that you are planning for contingencies, but more importantly, that you don't know everything!

Ask Questions

Solicit input from your crew. Not only do they have vital information that is required to achieve the mission, but they will respect much more if you go after that information.

CHAPTER TEN
The Enrollment: Is Everyone On Board?

Over fifteen hundred airplanes cross the North Atlantic every day, navigating via a set of five or six "tracks," which are plotted by oceanic control every 24 hours.   There are only a handful of diversion airports available for these aircraft, should an in-flight emergency arise. The weather at these "alternates" is sometimes terrible, with blowing snow, winds in excess of 35-50 miles per hour, and reduced visibilities. On the worst of days, only a very few pilots will be required to fly their passengers to one of these safe havens. On September 11, 2001, that all changed.

Hundreds of airplanes had to divert to these small cities in Northern Canada, Iceland, and Greenland — and they did it all at the same time! Within hours, these towns had to handle hundreds of aircraft, with thousands of people who would need basic services, such as food and shelter. Large amounts of fuel would have to be retained to refuel the jumbo jets. Schools would have to be converted to hotels, overnight!

Amazingly, the diversions worked out just fine. The designated alternate communities did a great job! There is however, one town that I would especially like to mention. It is the town of Gander, Newfoundland, located in the eastern province of Canada. This little town took care of thousands of diverting crews and passengers. They did laundry, cooked meals, opened their homes, and delivered meals to the airplanes. They also did something else. They printed up T-shirts that said "GANDER LOVES YOU!". This was above and beyond the call of duty. The passengers followed the Gander citizens because they trusted them. The Gander people became the Commanders under very difficult, and unimaginable circumstances. They led, and the guests of their community followed. People will not follow weakness, but they will follow strength.

Create a Safe Environment For Input

Set the tone for discussions by asking questions. Maintain leadership by acknowledging each input as being "valuable information." Log input to be reviewed later. Make eye contact. Smile. Listen!

Define Duties and Purpose

Direct your crew in the development of the team mission statement. The crew creates it, and The Commander verifies that it does encompass the mission at hand. Everyone counts. Emphasize — one crewmember can save the day or cause the crash!

The crew mission statement needs to be displayed where each crewmember can read it everyday. It is a visual reminder of not only the mission importance, but also of the crew's importance. When they deal with a large number of daily distractions, this mission statement will serve as a reminder of what they really want, after all, they wrote it!

CHAPTER ELEVEN
Accepting Command

There is a subtle difference between knowing you're right and thinking you're right. Understanding this difference is critical to effective leadership.

There was an early morning fog blanketing the Providence airport, as several flights were preparing to taxi from the terminal and line up for take-off. A 757 passenger-jet was landing on runway 5R, and was instructed to clear the runway, and then taxi to the gate. However, due to the low visibility, the pilots mistakenly turned back onto the active runway, while thinking they were on the taxiway leading to the terminal. The ground controller did not have visual confirmation of the 757 (because of the fog), and queried as to its location, only to be assured by the pilot, that they were actually on a safe taxiway. The controller then proceeded to clear a US Airways Metrojet for take-off on that very same runway. The US Airways Captain refused the clearance for take-off, maintaining that he would need better clarification as to the location of the 757 passenger-jet. The controller then proceeded to clear a cargo plane for take-off, which flew directly over the 757 on the runway, narrowly missing it. When asked why he would not accept the take-off clearance, the US Airways pilot responded that it was the inconclusive tone of the preceding ATC and pilot communications, and not the words that cautioned his take-off acceptance.

This pilot knew that the take-off would not be safe. He didn't just think he was right, he knew it. He knew it because he had maintained total situational awareness of his environment and had remained aware of the conversations through effective listening. He also knew that the spoken word accounts for a mere 7% of communication. Knowing you're right can only come from effective integration with your environment. Thinking you're right, possibly leading to a catastrophe later, is the result of insufficient integration and a lack of situational awareness.

Leadership and Followership

You have accepted the responsibility — accept the Command. Assign roles for the crewmembers — note-taker, timekeeper, etc... All roles are valued with specific duties but rewards will be team-based. Assertiveness is desired, aggressiveness is not allowed.

Situational Awareness

The Commander must maintain a state of situational awareness. As each crewmember is delegated the various tasks during the mission, the Commander will have the big picture. Obviously, the more data that each crewmember can handle, the lower the workload for the Commander. In effect, the Commander will watch over, coach and ensure all crewmembers are given the resources to complete their jobs. If the Commander micro-manages, due to fixation, distraction, or even ego — the loss of situational awareness will ensue.

Checklist

The Commander will verify that a dynamic, continuously updated, checklist is maintained. This can be delegated to the note-taker if desired. This checklist is created from the previous debrief, and follows both the master timeline, and the measurement system. It will give the team the ability to provide reliable performance during peak workloads, and prevent task overload. Additionally, tasks will be prioritized during the creation of the checklist, ensuring mission completion.

CHAPTER TWELVE
The Debrief

The debrief is an organized, systematic method of exchanging information related to the timeline, measurement system, and checklists that were in use. This is the opportunity to review, rethink, assess, and consider new methods or procedures if appropriate. It is not a blame game, a free for all, nor a pass-the-buck party. The Commander is in charge, however the crewmembers should feel free to request additional resources and support during this time. The Commander must leave the ego at home, allow open communications, and be receptive to the real data coming in from the "front lines." Consensus will be pursued, but not always realized. Ultimately, the responsibility rests with the Commander, and he or she will be accountable.

The Review

Note accomplishments of team as a whole. Acknowledge high performance as a group, and that of any individuals. Discuss team errors, such as timeline or measurement insufficiencies. Crew must share all pertinent data, but not opinions (at this point) with each other and the Commander. Commander must be receptive to data and be prepared to act on it.

Improvements

All crewmembers offer solutions to problems that were presented during the review. Consensus is the goal, fostering extremely creative environment. If consensus is reached — great! If this total agreement is not reached, Commander makes final decision, while accepting accountability, and everyone else gets on board. (In extreme cases, a number of crewmembers may need to take their case to a higher level.

Keep The Blue Side Up!

The primary flight instrument for a pilot is the attitude indicator. It displays the "attitude" of the airplane, and whether it is straight and level, with reference to the earth's surface. The bottom half of this instrument is brown — signifying the earth; while the top half of the display is blue — signifying the sky.

When you fly, you need to be right side up, have the proper attitude and stay on course. In other words - keep the blue side up!

82

CHAPTER THIRTEEN
Commander and Crew Courtesies

I was waiting with my wife in a room filled with more than a dozen other nervous patients. They were rightfully concerned as this was a facility where MRI's, mammograms, cat scans and similar procedures were performed to help diagnose their conditions. As with my wife, it appeared that most of them also had been advised by their personal physicians to promptly schedule this "non-routine" appointment. After waiting an hour beyond our designated time, my wife's name was finally called, and we approached the service window assuming she was to have her test. To our surprise, we were told that our insurance would not cover the cost of the testing. This was simply incorrect, as my wife actually has two insurance companies, both of which would cover all or part of the cost. To maintain calm in what was already a disquieting atmosphere, I quickly placed a call to our primary insurance company, verified the coverage, and gave a point of contact to confirm this fact to the staff member assisting us. This accomplished nothing. We were essentially dismissed. Of course this was not an option since we had waited several weeks for this appointment, and my wife's doctor had recommended taking action sooner rather than later. Seeing a VISA logo on the wall, I went so far as to offer payment on the spot and I'd take care of the insurance issue on my own. We were surprised again, when the staff member refused and suggested we try elsewhere. The entire experience was traumatic for my wife and exasperating for me.

At this point I realized that the overloaded staff person was fixating on the insurance issue, lost situational awareness with the customer, and had simply not been trained to recognize this Red Flag. She had completely forgotten that she

55

was the "gateway" to a room and a doctor, where a patient might learn of some very serious and personal medical conditions.

The issue was resolved shortly, with the manager and doctor getting personally involved. Situational awareness returned, the scans were completed, and we were on our way.

Fixating on certain aspects of their job, in a task-overload environment, caused these employees to lose their situational awareness. They could not see the big picture since they were focusing so intently on the smaller problem. This is not to say that the insurance issues did not exist; they were as real to the office staff as the gear light was to the previously mentioned L-1011 flight crew. It was part of their environment. It needed attention, yes, but not to the exclusion of the doctors' patients. If they had been trained to recognize the red flags, they could have recognized this common failure at an earlier point in the process.

Additionally, every Commander and crew must develop the routine practice of common manners. I call these the "**Commander and Crew Courtesies**," and they are expressed by the entire crew as part of the everyday culture. Courtesies build unity; it is that simple. They take all of our multicultural backgrounds and bring them to the same playing field, and further our sense of unity and common worth. They show respect for others before they "earn it." In other words you acknowledge "the good" in your fellow crewmember right from the start.

A lack of manners and courtesies, show a lack of respect for others and even oneself. This in turn shows a lack of self-confidence in oneself. Some people used to think that using courtesies and customs of respect meant that you did not honor another's uniqueness, and tried to conform them to some robotic standard. This could not be further from the truth! When you use the courtesies, you are saying to someone "I may not know of your uniqueness yet, but I respect myself, I will respect you as well." The following is an abbreviated list of **Commander and Crew Courtesies:**

The Face-to-Face Encounter:

• Give firm hand shakes (especially men)

• Make eye contact, smile

• Always mention "please" and "thank you"

• Offer "It is my pleasure" vs. "no problem"

• Use discretion with private client information, such as social security numbers, bank accounts, phone numbers, hotel rooms, etc...

• Open with, "How can I help you today?" or "How can I be of service today?"

• Offer, "I will be right back with your change."

• State, "I am sorry you are having a difficult time, may I try to help you?"

• Remember to send a "Thank You" note!

Do not:

• Employees do not use cell phones at counter, unless required for the job.

• Do not carry on conversations of personal nature (not related to the customer) at the service counter.

• Do not make comments that the "boss is wrong again," or that the other employees screwed this one up.

The Telephone:

- Answer the phone with "Hello, you have reached Family Chiropractic, this is Nicci, and how may I be of service?"

- Introduce yourself with, "This is Bob Johnson, the office manager for Johnson Groceries. May I speak with Tom Smith?"

- Answer with, "I'll check on that for you, may I put you on hold, while I see if your party is available?"

- Offer, "I'm sorry, Bob is not available, would you like his voice mail, or is there something that I can do for you?"

- State, "I will be happy to help you with that." Or "I'm sorry, I don't have the authority to do that, but may I transfer you to someone who does?"

Do not:

- Do not cut off the client mid-sentence.

- Do not leave a person on hold for more than a few minutes, without checking in with them.

- Do not talk to others, while the client is on the phone.

- Do not eat during conversations.

- Do not read aloud, in front of others, any secure information. (Social Security numbers, hotel rooms, bank account numbers, phone numbers, etc...)

As previously mentioned, the Commander and Crew Courtesies must exist throughout the entire team, as part of the professional culture. This will then provide an authentic representation of the company's true culture, and employees will not have to "put on a show." It is just the way it is, and it is that simple. As a result, hiring practices may improve over time, as will the expected customer base.

CHAPTER FOURTEEN
The Multi-Generational Workplace

Today's workforce is comprised of up to four generations: the Matures (pre-WWII era), Baby Boomers (1945-1964), Generation X (1965-1980), and the Millennials (1981-present). Each has its own distinctive behaviors, attitudes, language, interests, ethics, approaches, goals, and expectations. As a result, employees from different generations will respond better to varied types of leadership. The Commander and Crew model is effective across generational boundaries, and knowing a few facts about workplace demographics will help you be a more effective leader.

The Baby Boomers are the most numerous and will continue to dominate the workforce over the next decade. Newest on the scene, the Millennials already comprise a large group, about to outnumber the Gen X employees and rival the Boomers. The number of Matures in the workforce understandably continues to decline.

Values are a major area of generational distinction for these groups. The Matures, for example, subscribe to duty, honor, country, commitment, and hard work — THEN prosperity. The Boomers tend to have a different view — they ARE their job, and attach much personal worth to the titles and recognition they achieve. In the end, hard work always pays off — that's their motto! All they need is a vision or a goal and they'll be off, needing little direction, preferring an independent work-style. But rest assured, they get the job done!

The Gen X employees were the first group to be at ease with global technology. They experienced constant change, in their world and homes, which required them to adapt often. All this change made them crave high levels of honesty and trust in the workplace. Show them the money! They need to see recognition and reward early in the program.

Millennials are the new "baby boom," and their numbers in the workplace are on the rise, soon to exceed the original Boomers. Hence, they need to be known, taken into account, and most importantly — nurtured. At first sight, it appears that their adolescence has been extended by about 10 years. This is especially common in America, Europe, and Japan. This generation has been raised with much parental attention, and they have a genuine fondness for their families, so much in fact, that leaving home can become an issue. They gained high stimulation through toys, activities, and technology enabling them to think quickly though with shortened attention spans. Overall they are positive and have lofty goals; to achieve those goals, however, they need, and welcome, explicit direction. Be sure to give them a good plan, as they will follow it! Committing to a business entity for the long term is not on their radar, but they will seek individuals of high integrity and stick with them. If their supervisor lacks character, they will probably move on.

CHAPTER FIFTEEN
Faith

Ronald Reagan had a policy with the Soviets that was quite effective. He referred to it as "Trust and Verify." After the two parties would reach an agreement, President Reagan would inform Mr. Gorbachev that he trusted him to follow through on his commitment, and that the U.S. would follow through with the verification process. This was a new procedure, and some viewed it as a method which suggested we had faith in the Soviets, and others viewed it as a symbol of a lack of faith. I believe that it was a show of faith, and that it possibly saved the two countries.

When you have faith in someone to fulfill an agreement, you, in essence, trust them to come through. You are saying to them - "I expect that you will do this." This can take a tremendous amount of faith in some circumstances, and even more faith to check on the results and verify that it was done as agreed. When you have the courage to face the other party during the verification process, you are expecting the good (faith), and not running from the bad (fear of deception). This takes courage.

As a Commander, you will discover that you will need faith more often than not. You will dig deep into yourself and you will find it. You will be expecting to see the good in people. You will strive to see their integrity and honesty. You will articulate your expectations with focus, believing that the crew will follow through with their commitments.

You will discover that you not only have faith in your crew, but more importantly, in yourself.

References

Wiener, E.L., Kanki, B.G., Helmreich, R.L. Cockpit Resource Management. Academic Press, Inc., 1993.

Cockpit Resource Management Training, NASA Conference Publication 2455, Proceedings of a NASA / Industry Workshop, May 1986.

DeNucci, Peter. Captain's Discretion. Apollo Publishing, Ltd. 1996